IN THE KEY ⟍ ⟋ BLUE

Richard Lawson

New Generation Publishing

DEDICATION

To my family,

Nicky, Freya, Joe, Laurie, Virginia, Tabitha, Leda and Jessica

Thanks

To Brenda Salt for insisting that I made a book (sorry you never saw it).

To my friends especially Rosie MacDonald and Nina Tulloch for encouragement.

To Word Mustard in Weston, Open Mic at Halo in Bristol (as was), and Richard Carder at St James' Wine Vaults, Bath, for providing a microphone and audience.

Acknowledgments

These poems have been published:

Timeships: Coventry Prize

Scarborough Shore: Beehive

Night Call, The City Burns: Poetry Room (web)

Heaven watchers: Voice & Verse

Driving won first prize in the W-s-M based West Country Writers' Association

View from Crook Peak, Tsunami, A Wood in Somerset, Iraq, Leaves on the Lawn: Chickenbones http://www.nathanielturner.com/index.html

Drop, How will they live, Strange Light, A shadow touched, Down Changing Corridors, Fairground Ride: all in Nightingale.

Genoa, Lost Sock in a previous incarnation of Writers Hood.

The Dream: Poem of the Week in http://www.comrade.org.uk/

A Case of Fire published in Philosophy Now

The Fisherman, The Wild Horse: published in Aquarius many years ago

A Wood in Somerset, Iraq, and A Dream of War were judged joint third and highly commended (respectively) by Adrian Mitchell in the Iraq Occupation Focus / Red Pepper Poetry Competition 2004

To Walk Again was highly commended in the Iraq Occupation Focus / Red Pepper Poetry Competition 2005

Leaves: commended in the Partners Poetry Competition 2005

Biographical Note

These poems have emerged intermittently over the past half century in between my playing at medical student, hospital doctor, traveller, diver, psychiatrist, husband, father, walker, hang glider pilot, anti-pollution activist, Green Party district councillor and co-speaker, microlight pilot, inventor, sand yacht pilot, woodworker, bodger, blogger (www.greenerblog.blogspot.com), tweeter (@DocRichard), flautist, gardener and BrambleHook manufacturer.

More poems (including the quasi-mediaeval epic *Ogrin and the Boy*) can be found on my website www.greenhealth.org.uk.

Contents

LOST SOCK

I have just lost a poem
somewhere, in my thoughts.

it was short, but promising.
faint, like a dream.

poignant with a dash of acid.
I lost it behind that faint mauve line of hills

my mind is like an odd sock drawer

this one will have to do.

RETURN

If we could see that endless point in time
when we shall know for certain that
our journey here has reached its final end

and in some way   reel in the flow of life
and from that soaring pinnacle
look back upon this state

when we can live and love
and walk and breathe and
sing and talk and eat and act

and then   come back
remembering what we'd seen
no longer lost inside the crashing now

and now of world wave history
smashed in a broken compound eye
a shattered image of a breaking time,

then with that timeless vision
we'd live each golden heartbeat
with such fierce intensity

to drink the music of the sky
study the winding ivy on the branch
feel the excitement of the water in the stream

dance to the rhythms of the wave
and learn to live in such a way
that joy is everywhere.

TSUNAMI

Do not search hopelessly among the wreck;
not here, among the stench and sticks,
for those who left this heaviness behind.

They do not grieve, except for us
caught in the tangle of a broken paradise.
We search for what is not there in the wreck.

There is a mess of wood and broken stone
of silver bone and fertilising flesh.
They have done well to leave this weight behind.

They rise above a dark chaotic mass
moving to lightness from a hard, heart breaking work:
You will not find them here among the wreck.

For them the fear of death is in the past
from height they see the gasping shade of dark.
Their burden's gone; their being has grown light.

Look for your life among those who survive.
Wait patiently to meet the ones you seek.
Do not look now for them among the wreck -
for they have left their heaviness behind.

THE NOBLE LORD, LORD LAWLOR, LAUDS THE LAW

The Noble Lord, Lord Lawlor, lauds the Law.
He holds it vastly better than the law that held before.
He likes the lift in income for the rich across the board.
In many ways a modest, almost trivial award,
And he likes the Lamborghini that his lad can now afford.
                    (Haw haw)
The Noble Lord, Lord Lawlor, lauds the Law.

The Noble Lord, Lord Lawlor, lauds the law.
He deems it far superior to those laws they have abroad.
As for the lower orders, well he really was appalled
That anyone should cavil at what was after all
A just remuneration, not a licence to defraud.
The Noble Lord, Lord Lawlor, lauds the law.

LINES ON THE DEATH OF POPE JOHN
PAUL II

"No Popery" Ian Paisley cried,
and now that John Paul II has died,
there *is* no Pope,
so can we hope
for Orangemen with peace inside?

Nope.
They just can't cope
without a Pope.

The Papists need a Papacy
and Paisley needs an enemy.
Without a Pope
they'd all just . . . mope.

It really makes you think:
what if it pushed them off the brink ?
what if it made them turn to drink
or even . . . turn to dope?

Might be a blessing in disguise.
Imagine if the smokes that rise
above the Convocation
(as they all grope
for a new pope)
should symbolise a wider scope
for toleration?

What if the newly chosen Pope,
red-eyed, and reading Rattigan
loped lazily around the Vatican
flashing the peace sign,
Oh wow. Yeah. Wow. Yeah. Fine.

But that could be a slippery slope
No-one would want a hippy Pope.
We should not hope
for a doped pope;

But could we simply go for one
that has a decent sense   of fun?
Maybe when Ratzinger's gone?

A CASE OF FIRE

One day when I was working
Some smoke got up my nostril
I left my things and went outside
As fast as I was able.

When I got outside the door
A man in strange attire
Was pouring petrol on the floor
And setting it on fire.

"Oy oy ahoy hey hoy" I said
As matches scrape and rustle
"Don't burn my house, you'll burn my house."
He said "I've studied Husserl".

"You studied Husserl well so what?"
Said I with eyeballs gleaming.
He said "He says the house you got
With money, has no meaning".

Said I "Ah now I get your point,
You mean, to put it cleanly,
All meaning is invested in
The act of our perceiving".

"The act of seeing, yes that's right"
(With earnest knowledge teeming)
"The bricks and mortar catch alight
But not the house's meaning".

"But Neddy lad" I answered back
"The main point you're not grasping.
'twas Plato's ideals, not Husserl's
that were from everlasting".

"What do you mean?" he answered back
(but I could see it blinched him)
"You understand, you must" I said
"that change is now the lynch pin.

"Yes, change that all things suffer must"
(I stamped it on his cortex)
"Look at my house, you'll see it just
One great big flaming vortex.

"What once meant '*house*' right now means '*fire*'
Tomorrow will mean '*ashes*'
It's true that meaning can't be burnt
It's also true it changes".

"O gosh," he said, "I see it now,
I've been and burned it outright.
I must have misconstrued the text.
I really am most contrite".

"That's quite all right," I answered back,
"Experience is boxwood,
And I have just now come to learn
The usefulness of Oxford."

"Not Ayer's lot?" he said distraught
(For he could see my learning)
I said "Since Oxford comes to naught
It never comes to burning".

TEXT PLEASE

Don't you just love to text?
Only morons in shacks
fiddle round with a fax.

The ultimate fix
has come with a mix
of a phone and the clicks
on a back-lighted pad
that predicts and corrects
and also spell checks.

It's not just a fad
it's a leap for mankind.
You would find
that if Oedipus Rex
had been able to text
he'd have foiled the hex
that blighted his mind
and rendered him blind.

We can message at random
with merry abandon.
You know Posh and Becks?
I could send **them** a text,
'cept they're probably ex-
-directory, to avoid being vexed
with **millions** of texts.

The effects **can** be mixed:
though our digits get slick
it don't get us fit
'cos our pecs don't get flexed
while we sit on our bums
just twiddling our thumbs
updating our chums.

But who cares? I just love it.
If *you* don't, then shove it.
If you think you're above it,
no camera detects
your refusal to text
there's no Law (Latin: "Lex")
to insist that you do.
It's just up to you.
Don't want to? That's fine.
It's your loss, not mine.

But to addicts of text
it's better than sex.

OLD MACDONALD DID SOME HARM

The Big Mac
it's more than a snack
it's a smack
in the face
of the human race

not to mention the cow.
ow.

It's also a pat
on the back
of the almighty buck.

yuck.

all that gristle and fat
served up
in a bap.

look at the muck
in the gutters.
the packaging flutters
as a car goes by.

Why
can't they see
this is not the way to be?

Why
don't they know
this is not the way to go?

Hello?
Ever heard of Kyoto?
No?

They don't give a fack
about Iraq
not even about their heart attack
they just wanna snack
on a Big Mac.

IF YOUR MOTHER DOESN'T NEED YA

If your mother doesn't need ya
Get a job within the media.

Want to lie without redress?
Get a nice job in the press!

If you're regularly pissed
You could be a journalist.

If you like to cast ordure
You could be an interviewer.

If your thing is smearing poo
Broadcaster's the job for you.

If you'd like to be a Nazi
You can join the paparazzi

Don't let them fool you all the way -
Make April First your No News Day!

THE GIRL IN GREY

(After Fulke Greville)

Lost in Ladies Lingerie
In a store at Christmastide
Suddenly a Girl in Grey
Passes softly at my side.

Such a girl as pen forestalls
Such a face as brightens day
"Where," I ask "is Overalls?"
"Overalls?" she said "that way"

Then she pointed with her hand
Would have nestled in my palm
All my senses' fires fanned
White, her hand was cool as balm.

Stunned, I turn and walk away
Impelled where her finger showed
In her hand was light of day
And I swear the counter glowed.

Had the pointing finger bent
Loadstone I to her would fly
In a marriage with her blent
Never seen in Lingerie.

Lost in love at length I stop
At the counter where they sold
Overalls & Ladies' Smocks
Hung on hangers fold on fold.

There I waited for my turn
While the lady chattered on
How much shop assistants earn
What she should have said to Ron.

Fancy weaves itself a dream
Way above her clapping tongue
Drinking at a silver stream
Overhead by oaktrees hung

With a soft white form beside
Moving in a dappled shade
Ploughloam hair and satin eyed
On a couch of moss we made.

Then I saw – what can I say
Breaking in my reverie
Then I see the Girl in Grey
I had seen in Lingerie.

Men say dreams forewarn the man
Of a thing that time will bear
In a dream an angel can
Gather up a form of air.

Spirit forms delight the mind
Bodied forms give joy to sight
Both in one these two combined
Fear puts speech and sense to flight.

Shop girl eager and refined
Holds a smock up to her breast
"Was this what I had in mind?"
Brown eyes wide at my behest.

Millstreams that the weir has checked
Smooth in utter calmness lie
Happy merely to reflect
All that passes in the sky.

I a millpond to her sun
(Customers are always right)
Nylon, shapeless, colour dun
Over heartsdrum hear "Not quite."

Then she laughs and puts it back
Mournfully the hangers crunch
Smiling leaves me by the rack
And glides away to have her lunch.

Now the lady comes to me
Can she help in any way
Thinks I want Maternity
No I want the Girl in Grey

She a fast dissolving form
In a Christmas shopping nation
Lovely, witty, graceful, warm,
Lost through paslied hesitation

None will ever touch those hands
While he just adores and stands.

HEY TO SKATER

hey!

dancing on four wheels
down Park Street

I heard you
over the sounds of cars

Shalom!
Slalom!

live on like that
balancing courage with your skill

until you die.

NIGHT CALL

We share the night with foxes,
thieves, thoughts and milkmen.
We do not miss the day.

I've heard a blackbird
throw out a call of ecstasy
when the first blue gold of dawn
spread out an angel's wing around his form
etched in the sky above a darkened roof,

and it was life that sang to light
before the heat brought cloud and noise
and news of war.

LEAVING

I glance back as I leave the house
she's lived in all her life.
Now in half darkness, looking straight ahead.

Her only company is pain and
thoughts
        flicking
like birds in and out of an old hedge
like the ghosts in this ancient building
children who run and laugh for her in these dark rooms.

And when her son comes back, what can she say?
`The doctor came.
`My pain is less
`I thought of you,
`that time you fell out of the apple tree and cried`

IN A HOME

`Yes I'm all right'

the old one
turns away
towards the place
where all the old ones wait

not looking back

I caught
a lifetime's feeling
in her daughter's eyes

PHONEY DEATH

This phoney death
one long slow slide away
the folk you know
replaced by
    officers
charged with your care

fine as a china cup
slim as a junkie
impatient bones
shine through your limbs
and bowstring tendons crack

trapped in this failing flesh
wrapped in a stinking cloud
through which the faces of your caring gaolers
    drift
offering food, pills, painful
position shifts and sometimes,
    sometimes
a word, a smile, a human touch

NICOLA

You are my ally, patient friend and love
My anchor and my harbour in a storm
My ground below, and starry sky above
The wind that cools and sun that keeps me warm

I am the spark that dances on your flame
A feathered secd that floats along the air
A cloud that brings the dampness and the rain
That keeps your garden growing green and fair

Together we can live the best we can
Practice and learn the ways of being friends
Learn the deep secrets of woman and of man
Find out together how the story ends

Though fifty years have spun the astrolabe
For me, at least, you'll always be my babe.

POSTCARD TO VIRGINIA

Morning brings mist and sparkling woods
under white flags in naked sky

wish you were here

the water is in perpetual movement,
continually evades description

wish you were here

the surface of the water's never still
a huge heart heaves it to a complex dance

wish you were here.

Why try to describe the indescribable
that can be at one time
this glaucous fish-pregnant long drowned valley
a polished restlessness
and at another time
- at sea and under sail -
silver-sapphire
piles of power
trembling
and shivering in their own creator wind

and
where the footwork of our life shines bravely
first weightless
then landing on the back of this huge axe
scattering diamonds to either side
dancing on the dark blue void of airless watery
space
where

only fish can breathe

and
where you've lived for three long months
suspended
between air and ooze
with your companions pain
and a chorus of concern
when you can raise the strength
to open up your eyes from restless sleep

pulled by our love
drawing you back to pain and struggle
to make you work on this crashed vehicle

still beautiful
your smile a rising sun casting aside the clouds
and mist
in this world where we can eat and play together

wish you were here.

THE SHED

To Rudolph Lewis

I hope that you, old friend, toiling away
to fix the roof of your store shed
all day for days in overwhelming heat,
the sweat of natural Florida,
that makes this too-warm English summer
seem temperate again,
I hope you win. I hope your father's store
Is gloried with the roof   that it deserves
I hope that you don't fall.

I want my friends in Africa
pinned down in Mogadishu
by flying lead, not nails,
to know about your shed.

I want as many people now
to know about your shed
as stand to learn from it,
because it's more than shed
we talking here.

Fine as it no doubt is   as shed,
this one is more than timber,
more than tar paper and sweat,
more than determination,
more than a health and safety risk,
more than some slabs of wood
arranged with more or less regard
to canons of structural integrity:

It is a thing of spirit,
creation of a living poet.

Architecture. Frozen blues, maybe.
Cathedrals come to mind.

Not that they should come
en masse to make a pilgrimage,
although in fact when you have gone
they might well come,

for few are famous while they breathe,
and of the ones that are,
it would be better for us all
that some were not,
                                    maybe.

The point is that this shed
is getting built.

Trees are our brothers.
They live and die
just like John Barleycorn,
and willingly give up the sap
to win new life in service to their family.

This shed was once alive,
bi-placentate, a joiner-up of earth and sky
the fusion point in its green sap
to all four elements.

Like Shiva's locks that broke the flood
Its leaves gave shade from blazing sun.

Trees give us unconditional love,
like dogs and gods;
                    some gods,
                                    sadly not all.

It died to find itself becoming shed.

Frozen blues? In Florida now
the only frozen things
are found in white machines
humming beneath their breath
just while the juice is on.

Not frozen: solid blues
from far away, blown out by Buddy Bolden,
crossing a river wider, deeper,
cooler than Pontchartrain
to celebrate one poet's work.

It's up there with the wolf and owl
and in the end, I dare say
up there with
Eli, Eli Lama Sabacthani,
if all the Truth be known.

The point is this:
this is a shed that's going *up*.
Rudy is in the business of building sheds,
not breaking them.

He does not use his strength to knock down sheds.
He does not bulldoze structures.
He brings no lethal force to bear   on others' work.
There are no bombs in Rudy's bag.
That's all. That's good. That's all we need.

SCARBOROUGH SHORE

It is essential that I stand   here at the water's edge
    watching the waves wash over silky sand.
    I must commit this sight to memory
though I have been here now so many times

It is important, time is conspiring
    to rob me of this ancient vision
    the tide is ebbing, and still I do not know
how that smooth wave

will grow, and crest, and fall
    and hiss its foaming feathers at my feet.
    I cannot see its essence, only the form
And memory of other waves.

It is important that I stand here,
    facing the simple line where sky and sea
    merge in infinity; stand here
in this domain where sea melts into land;

stand at this margin, unchanged since
    our living world condensed
    out of the crucible of energy
that is the breath of Spirit.

Stand with my back towards
    those children darting from pool to pool
    touching with round red hands
the coldness of the endless sea

Turning my back upon that seaside town
    Its hollow walls, wasp nest with sharper lines,
    giving a fair pretence of permanence
but stained with salt-rust, and its footings cracked.

I am compelled to stand here watching
    trying to learn, remember, trying to sense.
    For we shall pass, the sea
will stay.   And hidden in the shorebreak

There is a revelation surer than any teaching,
    if only we could hear. The Infinite is here
    Breathing again and again one word
Sssshhhhh........

TIMESHIPS

Spoken by a seventeenth century seaman

Many times when I laid down my head
and my old limbs were granted stillness,
in that instant before plunging into dead sleep,
the flitting lightness between shipboard and water,

in that timecrack before rocking into
re-dreams of days steeped in the presence of Death,
when my only hope was the captain
and the captain's only hope was God,

be that God his own damned self, or else
the science and art of his seamanship
or even, when those hopes drowned in the last wave
the God of his mother;

I felt that ancient unworked hope of peace
when the sea was out to kill you
when instant obedience is salvation
from having saltwater whistle in your lungs.

In that hair thin moment I felt Presences
people with limbs like us clad in
strange clothes and driving swift shining ships
that whip along carrying no cargo

except the cargo all but orphans carry,
the burden of love for family and home.
Many have felt them at some time
though none of us know why they sailed.

Some say they went for sport,
to have the sea wash out their souls
like well fed lords who hunt when there's no need,
making their hunger as they hunt.

I'll not believe that any man faced the wave's crack
for play. To me they're gods or angels
come back to talk to our old souls
and maybe touch and help us.

LOOKING BACK

Sometimes I get a pint of gas
and use a drop to drive around the block
just like old times, just for a laugh
but that is less and less. Soon it will stop.

I hear they've got it worse
in other parts.
Back here at least we have a fertile earth
and stronger hearts,

but there we hear they fight.
For food
but even all their riots
go off half cock. It does no good.

Back in the day
we'd waste more   in a single meal
than some of my grand-children's mates
eat in a week.

It's not as if we didn't know back then.
There were a few quiet voices,
but shouted down by money men,
who influenced our choices.

Their advertising lights
were bigger than your biggest store,
letters across the night time sky
why we should buy some more.

We didn't have no famines way back then.
Most people lived to see old bones.
I never saw a stiff 'til I was ten.
Death only visited old peoples' homes.

Aye, they were happy times.
Too happy. How I regret
we never pulled the lines,
never slowed up the horses of our greed.
We should've taken a bit more heed
we should've kept a bit of seed,
not treated you, our children, with such blind neglect.

HELFORD RIVER POOL

Satin silk and velvet
are rougher than the surface of this pool
on this evening of silence
and beautiful echoes
echoes

we come in sleek ships
trailing canned music
like a dustcart trailing flies

a hunter pops the silence

we swing at peace
on an island of human tools and toys

to be so bathed in darkness
that words vanish into the page
like whispers in a storm.

When our dream ends
this water, this rock, this hill
and this old wood
remain

our life flies like a bird
following the tranquil air downstream
revelling in the slow smooth slipping away

within
without
silence

silence
curlew
curlew

the hunter's gone

just music now

the fisherman
            placid by the sea
his line still and deep
calling up
            what silver memories

the wild horse
           brown eyes turned down
choosing its sudden path
          quiet dignity
among the stampede each horse
a lagoon of quietness under the passing storm

SEVERN ESTUARY

Sick, she shines bravely
slops muddily on rocks
smiles through her pain

too tired to be angry
desultory splashes
a trollop's dishwater.

elsewhere
the sea is emerald,
heaving, transparent.

Here, it's a salty soup
lightly seasoned
with industrial waste

thickened with good Gloucester soil
fecund but delicate
leaving the farm for ever

to drift and dull the waters
and be laid down and in a little while
come back as shale.

In our brief time
between erosion and petrifaction
we make the best of it.

PRAYER FLAG

Ragged as a wizard's beard
     and blown white hair
some fronded   plastic
     dresses the sharp buds of a sleeping tree
beside Trawsfynydd lake.

A prayer flag.

And the prayer :-

"Lord Mammon, hear us.
"We do not care for Nature, but for You
"Who are the juice that flows
"From Nature's wounded side,
"And for the goods You give
"To be our own possession
"To have and to hold
" 'Til Death us do part
"For ever and ever
"Amen."

UNLESS

Each spring   brings peace and hope.
The being of things   points to coming times
and every thin green leaf
contains a crowd of meaning.

Each leaflet puffs itself to shape
just like an insect's wing unfurling
and within
assembles perfect latticeworks.

Each net contains one single jewel
perfect in size and properties
to resonate in just   such a way
in sunlight. Transforms the energy

shot from the single sphere of fire
so that it can link gases to make sweetness
and send its sugars out: some to the roots
to power their never ending search

through the dark earth feeling for tiny jewels,
some to the wood, to bring it closer to the sun,
and some to fruit, so that the sweetness
promised by blossoms now, in Spring,

will feed its brothers, out of plenitude
graciously. And in return, we spread the seed
and nurture it.

And so the Spring is good, and all the codes for this sweet ritual
go forward *(unless)* clothing this valley, and the next,
clothing the hills *(unless)* clothing the Earth
in a living cloud-like green protective mantle.

The promise is there. It's strong.
Things change. Wars end.
Pendulums swing. Waves rise and fall.
Phoenixes may arise.
Spring can return.

Unless

THE VALLEY'S ANSWER

This valley, brilliant now in May sunshine
has raised generation after generation
of sturdy children, knowledgeable of
what is to be ate, and what is not.

Strong-legged along old winding lanes
each with some favourite corner
where in one bright and drowsy afternoon
Nature strikes their heart, and theirs alone

as one leaf, one stone,
one flashing grain of silica
captures their mind
anchors it in the One

until, unless they die, they grow to lusty adulthood
and chase and kiss and marry and
raise more, all feeding off
the fertile valley soil

that's still there, thinner now maybe
maybe the buds and butterflies are less
and more and more needs feeding to the soil
to win the food, but still

Wave after wave; young, parents, old
and passed away. The rich green valley
churns them steadily; they're good folk
hard-working for their food, they dance and sing.

Every few years, the military come
and tell their stories, show off their uniforms
and spirit away, playing their pipes and drums,
some young men to the wars.

A few come back, that long look in their eyes,
that absence; others more clearly missing
an arm, a leg, and eye, a mind.
Others do come back never.

They leave a dank cold shadow across their lover's life
someone who might have been; a husband,
one who does not flare up in nightmares
doesn't lash out for no good reason

one who was taken by the wars
and there are hot dark tears
and sadness clothes a young maid's life
and anger, always at the back

deep and unspoken. 'Why did he have to go and die?'
and always back that wave of common sense,
chorus of voices everywhere
'There always will be wars'

Tearing at her persistent inner voice
Why did he have to die?
Until the valley says
"I'll raise you, over and over, wave after wave

I'll give enough for you to eat,
and what's left over, goes to market.
Won't that do for an answer?"

Maybe not.

MOUNTAIN RESORT

Here where the mountain peaks
melt into cloud

and the light is brilliant
on Hockney pools

when for a silver second
the diver's spark hangs in the air

and the sound of voices
laps like trapped water

and thin music breaks the stillness
like a wasp's insistence

in dry heat we lose ourselves
wallowing in sunshine we have made mordant

our skin sleek, shining, soft
and slowly withering

our images grow thin
like mountains fading into haze

or colour washing from a photo
turning it all to sickly blue,

we rest and wait in short shadows
waiting for warm evenings

waiting for sleep and for the morning
waiting for time to pass

until our life unfolds
its reel of memories

hoping to find
a diamond on the pool's aseptic floor

SEPTEMBER 11 2001

This footage beats the best of Hollywood
a sudden bloom of cancerous fire
and smoke, the beating of a million black wings.

Obsessively we watch the symbol of the modern dream
collapse in stark fragility, a house of cards;
the highest order falls to fiery hate

And you my sister, brandishing that scarf
'I'm here,' balancing height and heat
until you chose the sheer sharp flight

We can not see the rush of startled souls
not hear the too long groans of pain and fear
until sweet sleeping death crept over them

And yes! You'll be avenged! More sons
will die, more mothers scream and raise their hands
to an avenging God. We cannot stop the world.

It has to be like this. We're only human after all.
This is reality - not film.   Justice and reason -
that's just a childish dream.
Think what you're told to think.

A WOOD IN SOMERSET, IRAQ

Stone still   in opalescent air
trees wait supportively.

Light splinters on new leaves.

Sun for the seventh day
blesses an English spring.

Two thousand lives away
this anticyclone fires up a storm
that drowns a nightmare world
in ochre light.

The peace I feel
leaning against the powerful grey fist
that grips the earth, cushioned with moss,
back shaped, kind as an elephant,

finds its reflection in a furious world
of men who sleep walk,
fall on their mother's skin,
give screaming fire,
act and react,
but cannot take it in.

Birdsong fills my head,
sharp as the sunlight
sparking on those tiny points of green.

One hammer headed woodpecker,
knowing no better and no worse,
fires off his rounds.

I should be suffering,
but the paper world is folded at my side,
its front page images of death
have left off stirring
in this gentle air.

OCCUPATION: JOBBING SQUADDIE

It's what we're trained to do, it's just our job.
If jumped up Hitlers want to get tooled out
with nukes and gas and germs that they can lob
at us, we'll bring them down, no fuckin doubt.

It wasn't so much warfare as a rout.
The worst our unit faced was sand and heat.
Talk about open doors - if we got out
to piss, they'd stick their hands up. They were beat.

It wasn't really such a major feat,
it's just our job, it's what we're trained to do.
First they were friendly, nice as you could meet.
We all relaxed. Nobody had a clue

how it would all go sour. Nobody knew
exactly when   we overstayed our leave,
but when a roadside bomb took out our crew
I got the first faint sus we'd been deceived.

We didn't mind the looters and the thieves
we're trained for that, it's all part of the job.
The thing that always makes my stomach heave
is facing down a screaming angry mob.

Stones hurt, bottles can burn, but when they gob
and spit at you, that is the thing...
we sweated blood   to save the fuckwit yob
who's screaming hate at you...it's that what stings.

We chased and caught them. Some one brings
them back inside the compound walls.
I heard our sarge say "Make them sing".
We laid in with our toecaps on their balls.

We got court martialled. Told us all to crawl.
Told us what not to say, gave us a gag.
They called it torture. I say we lost our rag.
We'll pay with years for one five minute brawl.

What stupid bastard sent us to this war?
How is this supposed to help the British nation?
They lied to us - we're here for Bush's oil.
No paddle in a shit-creek situation.

Two years have passed since liberation.
There were no WMD. That lying slob
Blair, he fouled up. This is an occupation.
He should jailed, not us. It's not our job.

THE PROMISE OF HIROSHIMA

It was all so beautiful.
Mathematics could dissect reality itself,
Complex, and finely balanced,
A logan rock that moves with just a touch,
and through these mysteries
we came to understand
the energy constrained within a grain of sand.

Infinitesimal becomes
unbounded power.
One plane, one flash
One whole town gone to dust.
Nothing except a few skeletal lines
Some shadow where a man had been.
Silence, apart from screams.

For some, that was success.
And this is how it stays. We live
under the sword of Damocles
death dangling by a hair,
our fallibility denied.
We live beneath the constant threat,
our wilful ignorance of hell.

As if the sheer perfection of the science
could purge the politicians' faults.
As if the discipline
that led them to unlock the door
could somehow spread itself
into the corrupted soul and mind
of those whose stock in trade is lies.

NIGHTMARE IN GAZA

One child's face
pressed up against his mother's cheek,
cold and indifferent
to the blazing of her grief.

Cold as the war machine
that ordered up this kill.

WE WHO ARE ABOUT TO DIE

we from our dusty streets

who in markets loud with the colour of nature's gifts

are looking with brown eyes from folds of muslin

as we go about our daily lives

to fill the leaky basket of our children's needs

so that they do not die,

salute the deadly gifts

you share with those we love

more than you understand.

HAIL TO THE CHIEF

You flash this filthy flower, this red pustule
with foul black winding sheet that is your final word.

This is your moment of fulfilment,
your argument that cannot be denied,

since everyone who sees this rose of death
is forced to feel the hate that tortures you.

It echoes on and on in desolate triumph
a set of images caught in facing mirrors

trapped in a split infinity : hate, hurt,
hurt, hate, irrational regress, endless,

your wasted world, where nothing grows,
no bird sings, only a lacerating hate

that stains your too-committed consciousness,
the perfect canvas of your world, with blood of babes,

and us, the bystanders, no longer innocent,
spattered with hate.

We feel a surge of hate for you, and so it goes
over and even until death, which does not part us,

until the pity that we feel for your split victims
can grow and blossom into a piteous love that swells

to cover the whole world until it swallows even you,
you pitiful child-leader, engulfing you in

pain-struck, hate-contaminated love,
the leader who in some way we have allowed

through lifetimes of inattention, to speak and act for us,
to mouth these foul excrescences, these blasphemies

against the Life that bears us,
to speak these bombs on our behalf .

We powerless to pity you enough, rightly to pity your pain,
condemned to heal or share your nightmare

until we die.

GENOA 2001

Cubic, fist sized
the black bloc offers
concrete poems
speaking violence to power

Phallic, rib cracking
the Law hacks out a harsh rejection slip
on sleeping forms
of those who fight
with dreams, not rocks or clubs.

Twelve thousand years
evolved this final script,
prologue and epitaph
of primate history

CAUGHT IN THE CROSSFIRE

Caught in the crossfire
crouching beside your father
behind the rubbish bin
until a slug untied the fragile knot
that held you in this dusty unkind world.

You soared to paradise I'm sure
but paradise is often tainted
with anger dripped out from martyrs'
wounded souls.

Some scars don't heal.

Oh, we can give, and grieve
and hold each other
and hate, or block it out
or turn our minds to other things
but this is where we sit:

caught in the crossfire

DREAMING IN KHAKI

I lived through a dream one night,
Beginning in the usual way, a group
Of people on some common task

Gathered on the beach
Lit by a fire, within a darkness,
Needing for one of them to die

"I'll do it" said my dreaming self,
Impulsive, eager to please

And so I died - something involving waves
Khaki green shorebreak, others were there,
That memory is vague,

But not the vivid beauty of a breaking day.
A dawn that reached out from the west
A hollow vibrant violet coral light
The surface of a sapphire seen from within
Taut as a bowstring
Splitting the world of darkness.

I was laid out in the mud
Feeling the dawn, not cold
Until a mother came,
Bent down, and looked at me.
"Poor boy" she said, speaking to herself

Then walked away

DREAM OF CONFLICT

If the red slayer thinks that he kills...

Two partisans about to die
suck on dry rags
call for water
and more bullets for their store

And if the victim thinks that he is slain...

To the North
Ganesh dances carefully
swinging his dusty blue trunk
above a child.
lucky beginning

they are mistaken...

To the south
two policemen
in best community manner
casually distribute letters and pleasantries,
as if to say
"Why not turn your muzzles to your mouths
save us the time and trouble?"

for the eternal in man cannot die...

But they have earned their choice of death
out of a lifetime of oppression
and in this film that changed into a dream
they wait out their last few minutes
bounded by unforgiving grey walls, litter
broken glass, and outside, to the north,
the elephant headed one,
and to the south, the emissaries of their death.

The spirit of Christ ...

Just now, they're sails becalmed, swinging, useless.
Waiting for the onslaught of noise
that gives them point and purpose,
turns on their power.

The heart bursting of the mothers son
their enemy, this strange love,
rod to rod until they feel the numb red comfort of
nemesis thudding into their flesh
to wake them from the dream of life.

...will never move us

It all began a while ago,
In dusty, endemic, common callousness
Played day by day, the way it always does.

*...to fight and war against any man with outward
weapons...*

FORBIDDEN

It is forbidden
To take the redolent soft clay,
The sweet warm excrement you made
Mould, smear and use it as your paint.

Wait 'til you are a man.
Then you can spray
The whole wide world with effluents of your trade
And live a life of wealth, success and fame.

It is forbidden
To hit your sister if she spoils your game.
Not even if she knocks your castle down.
You must not make her cry.

Wait 'til you're a man.
Then you can strike a living town
Send countless children to a silent grave
And be described as "brave".

It is forbidden.
Stupid boy! You must not play with fire.
I've told you many times that fire means pain.

When you become a man
Then you can plan to burn a million lives
And argue that's the only way
That peace can be maintained.
For that, they'll call you wise.

SYMPATHY FOR DEATH

To you
Whose head is red with stones
I bring you peace

To you
Whose lungs are filled with foul flood-water
I bring you peace

To you
Whose skin is licked with agonies of flame
I bring you peace

To you
Whose limbs and flesh are torn with energetic lead
I bring you peace

To you, small one,
Whose belly swells with lack of food
I bring you light and blessing.

To me
Met with universal fear, there is no peace,
Just knowledge of the way things are.

HOW WILL THEY LIVE

How will they live, our children
when like us they put their little ones to bed
and feel the lightless air
rich with cicadas   and the voice of dogs?

DROP

trembling in the gutter

a bougainvillea blossom

lies by a castoff yoghourt pot

if I fell off a cliff

there would be plastic by my corpse

THE FATE OF ROSES

When in the summer garden,
white roses spread thin snow across the path
    time fails

when in the bursting hedge
dead elms point leafless fingers at the sky
    hope falters

when in the silky sand of childhood's beach
the rusty barbs
    intended to hold invaders
    flapping like ravens to be shot
tear up the dancing foot
    innocence is less

when in the bowl of lights
those heads appear
    exchanging streams of words
    which avidly avoid
time, care and hate
    truth fades away.

I'll take the fate of roses

RUNNING FROM SURT

We travelled North
away from breathless heat
and blood red rock
that pours out of the earth,

across great plains, past mountains,
we picked our way through forests
threaded by silver streams,
always our backs toward the heat

into a sweet white cooler world
until the ache of hard dark cold
consumed our infants and our sick
and turned us back.

We settled here,
where water was plentiful,
where mountains breathe out mist,
not choking fire

and here we stayed,
here where the gentle Vanir rule
where the good light is by
but does not burn

here where the ice and fire
sway gently to and fro, like waves
or tide, and where the mist
flows from the cattle's breath

where innocence is all,
and good is in the rocks and streams and
field and food and friends and family
and here we stay

until the final fire comes to us from the South.

MIDAS

The Thames' flat scales reflect

a sky of gold

that freely gives

much more than City men

could ever hold

LEAVES ON THE LAWN

This happens every year.
Coloured and sculpted to look like frogs
a leaf-plague crawls across the mossy lawn,
sometimes by hop and skip, mainly by stealth.

Blurring the borders
blanketing mournful flower beds.
Their plan is simple: cover the earth with mulch,
rot-fragrant brown leaf drifts,

repeat each year
make a fine soft nursery for seedlings
to raise their heads, spread out their arms to greet the sun
and in their turn, drop leaves.

We cannot criticise.
Within our species there are those
who'd clad the earth in death
without a thought.

Between those two extremes
we have to set distinctions.
Grass here, flowers there,
and leaves in shining sacks

to wait three years,
rot down to fibre, to make soil.
Improvements that I may not see,
if in my turn I go to ground, the land sold on

maybe to be covered yet with concrete death
or reclaimed by the river.

but we must do this work ;
                             our given role
is to improve our soil and our soul.

STANDING OUT

(for heroes of the continuing Resistance)

Sheets and shards of colour
bleed from the dying sun
but they are lost to us,

as we are lost, and far from home.
The path has gone, each step
a foot placed into the unknown,

a stumble on hard rock.
Darkness has closed in
a gas mask with no air

stinking of vomit and black fear.
That simple threat :
say what you know, or die.

Closed off from ever present air
held back by the infinity
of thin black rubber and a deadly will,

so dark now, waves of black
throb with each desperate heartbeat,
each chill with fear, so far from home

no breath, nothing to see.
Speak. Say to him what he wants.
Courage has brought you here,

there's nothing more to prove,
and look, above the rock,
the bruising weight of earth

there on that faint line
where the sun lays down
the Evening Star stands still,

and look too, one by one
first with great names,
Sirius, Arcturus, Aldebaran

and in their patterns
known, half known, and lost,
the Bear, the Lion, the Dragon,

Winged Horse, the Giant
with his club, and then,
in a firework crackle

stretched across the magnificence
of space   brilliant
outstanding, immovable, faint

standing against the black,
because of darkness
the universal lights stand out

their shout - being and energy,
their song – soft, low,
inaudible yet sweet their music

promising that darkness is
a temporary loss of that which
underpins
        all being.

A ROUTINE DAY

It was a routine day
the way to work
marked out by sameness.

Packed up like cattle in a truck
we're all at pains to hide our shared humanity
like extras in a film,

strangers, obscure, unknown to anyone
apart from family and friends
apart from those who'd cry when we are gone,

apart from millions
who register a slender shock
to hear what happened next.

A flash of soundless light
changed everything, forever.
Bad editing, a jump,

or in a dream,
where brown and red
can shift around,

and no-one registers a thing,
not for a second,
not 'til the pain cuts in.

Then it was noise of fear and pain
the bellowing of cattle
worse than an abattoir

much worse than when we kill to eat
goats, sheep and cows.
Why not just line us up

Go there, strip off, breathe in and die.
Why not that ordered Nazi neatness
To reach their goal?

Why tear us all apart like spoiled brats
who rip their toys and throw red paint
to get their way?

And yet I know that I'm the lucky one
to have a heart that beats
to spite that empty space below my knees,

although each time my eyelids close
somehow the pinkness of the filtered light
conjures up images of tortured flesh,

just torn up flesh,
no more no less.
Halal or hamburger,

I do not care

Whether the author of our pain
is now in heaven with a thousand virgins
or laughing in his mess with brother officers

I do not care

Or screaming in hell while demons
with exquisite pains
put him together carefully

I do not care

Or in the highest office in the world,
bathing in lies
drowned in hypocrisy

I do not care

You who can freely walk the streets
You do the caring.
I only want to walk again.

ST CATHERINE OF BRUSSELS

Legend of shining beauty
Of sparkling intellect, deep learning
And perfect faith, the kind that leads to death,
Be with us now.

Although the house they built for you
Once gleaming white, is clothed in grime
With streaks of soot climbing the walls
Pray for us, Catherine,

Even if your windows' ironwork
Is turning brown, and your great doors are locked
And heavy lorries pass you by,
Indifferent,

Adding their mote of blackness
To your walls, and to our soft grey lungs
Shaking our eardrums and your stones.
Pray for our filthy souls.

Although you never did exist
Save as a paragon of faith
Exemplar of the power of Truth
Pray for us, holy saint.

You whose keen wit cut through
The sentences of slaves of power
The halitotic rantings of Maxentius' priests
Until they bowed

Bowed to your sweeter reason
One by one, came over to your side
So that the tyrant, smelling treason
Issued

His own short sentence that would
Liberate their souls from servitude,
That simple way the tyrant has
To save his world,

Slicing through the Gordian knot
Of theologians' necks, where blood
Speaks the immeasurable mystery
Of life itself.

And then he scourged your silky back
Imprisoned you, and when his wife
Came to you, and believed, she too
Was not spared death.

We know now that all this was
Myth making, legend, fairy tale.
We know you never broke the wheel he made
To break your spine.

No sharp sword sheared your beauty
And stilled your red persuasive tongue.
But we know too by their foul breath
Tyrants live on.

We know that through we left your side
Escaped the confines of your church,
Broke free of dogma, saw through the myth
We're still not free

of tyranny that still has
Lethal power, this time not simply over those
Who live within their boundaries
But over all the world.

Now all the world must always
Suffer and die, at the dictators' whim.
Although they have no throne, no presence,
Yet their rule

Is everywhere. Wherever
There is greed, they set up shop.
They've built their palaces
Within our minds.

So Catherine, though we left your side
Although your doors are locked
Although we treat you with neglect
Still pray for us.

STORM SHELTER

They say that rain's like tears.
What do they know?

I've seen real rain
run down the faces of my friends

while they laughed and cried
with playful happiness

to greet the huge warm drops
splashed down from
                        - not clouds

if these grey slops are clouds -
                        from bulging
dizzy uproarious pregnant
white blue-black grey light-shot
sky mountains. How do they know

there are no gods in there?
What does a man of any colour know of gods?

Those trembling raindrops
turned tawny dust a bloody brown

and in a lightning flash (it seemed to us)
the magic world turned green.

That's rain. This isn't rain.
It's more like a cold sweat

like the one drawn out when you
wake from nightmare

and fear to sleep again
in case you go back in.

But this is worse, the nightmare carries on
under the sun. You're caught both ways.

Instead of thunder
we got bombs

instead of flames from dry thorn sticks
crackling to warm a calabash of stew

we got the spitting fire
of small-arms battle noise

and all that sunlit
brown skin life joy stopped.

This cold thin silver greyness
is not tears. Tears are hot.

Faces that shone with rain
went still as stones, eyes now forever dry,

open in blank surprise,
and dead teeth shining

cloud white in faces pillowed
in brown skin mother mud.

The sun forever left my land
only the burning stayed.

Dreamlike we travelled,
ran, hid and waited until

somehow that moment
when the big bird roared and pushed

and I was born again
borne off the rumbling roughness of the ground

smooth into sunlit white-cloud world
where gods live for a day

to wake up
                    here

stood on a tarry Bristol road
polished with streetlights

crashing with cars
cold water running down my face

caught here alone, alive
but in a cold dark hell.

Of course, it doesn't always rain.
Sometimes I see a spark of good in someone's eyes.

Lightning Source UK Ltd.
Milton Keynes UK
UKOW01f2044120917
309070UK00001B/111/P